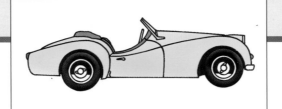

# THE
# A-TO-Z
# BOOK
# OF CARS

## ANGELA ROYSTON
## TERRY PASTOR

BARRON'S
New York · Toronto

# Alfa Romeo

**Aston Martin Vantage Volante 1979**

### Alfa Romeo Spider Veloce 1980

Although this Italian sports car was first built over 20 years ago, it is still sold today and is holding its own among more modern cars. The famous Alfa Romeo badge is based on the emblem of Milan, where the company began more than 80 years ago.

**Audi 80 1990**

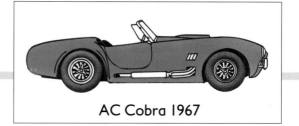

**AC Cobra 1967**

Bugatti

Bentley Mulsanne Turbo 1989

### Bugatti 35 1924

This Italian racing car was first built over 60 years ago. It won many races, including the World Championship in 1926. The Type 35 was made both as a racing car and as a sports car. The engine was started by turning the crank at the front. The spare wheel was strapped to the side.

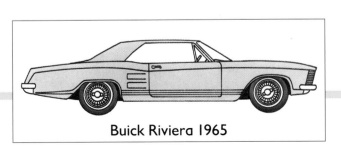
Buick Riviera 1965

BMW 635 CSI 1985

# Chevrolet

Citroen 2CV 1949

**Chevrolet Corvette 1984**
First produced about 40 years ago, the Corvette was America's first sports car. Although today's Corvette still has a huge and powerful engine, it is lighter than it looks because its body is made from fiberglass and plastic.

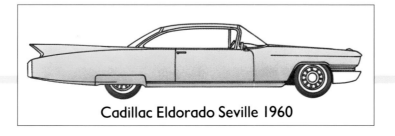
Cadillac Eldorado Seville 1960

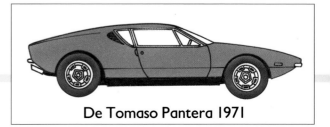
De Tomaso Pantera 1971

# Duesenberg

## ERA D Type 1936
The letters ERA stand for English Racing Automobile. This company was set up over 50 years ago to make English racing cars with small engines. Many of these models are still raced today in events for historic cars. The special suspension at the front helped the car go around corners faster.

## Duesenberg SSJ 1934
Only two of these sleek American luxury roadsters were made nearly 60 years ago. They were elegant and expensive then, and now they are worth more than $1 million each.

Datsun 260 Z 1976

# Ferrari

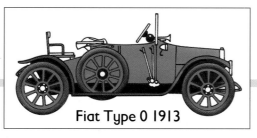

Fiat Type 0 1913

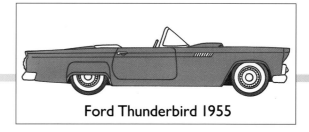

Ford Thunderbird 1955

### Ferrari Testarossa 1989
Testarossa is Italian for "red head." The car is called this because the cylinder heads in the engine are painted bright red. The slats on the sides are extra radiator grilles.

**Ford Anglia 1962**

# Gilbern

Hispano-Suiza Type 68 1935

**Gilbern GT Mk1 1959**
Gilbern was a small Welsh company that made cars for only 14 years. This two-door car was made about 30 years ago. Buyers assembled it themselves from a kit containing all the parts.

Honda Acura NSX 1990

Hudson Commodore 8 1950

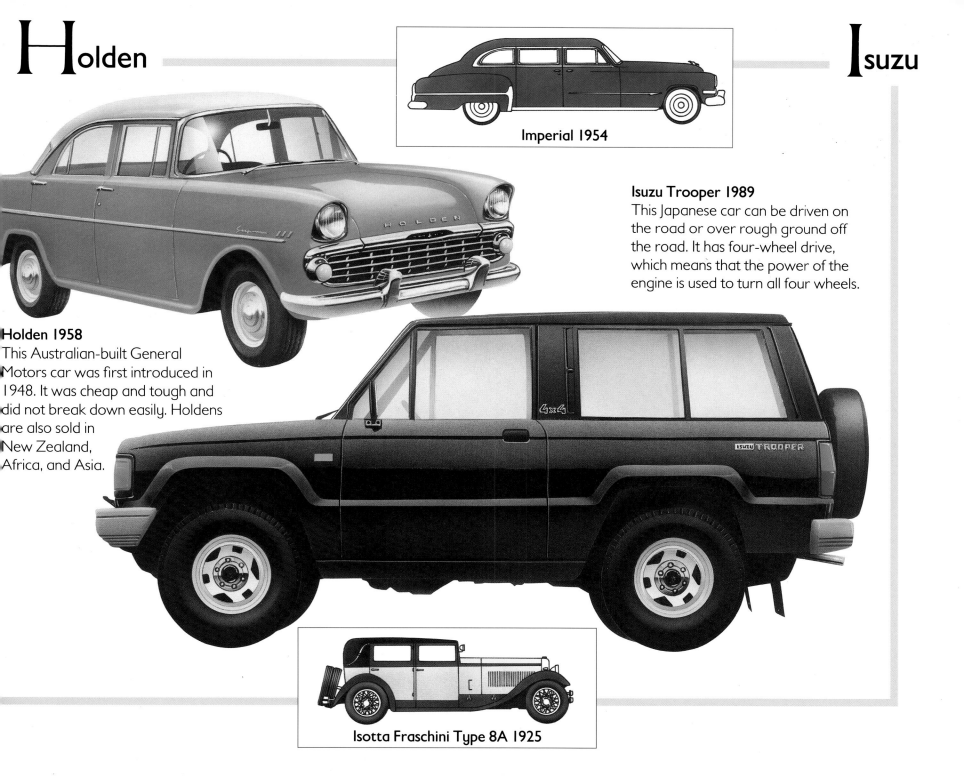

# Holden

# Isuzu

**Imperial 1954**

**Isuzu Trooper 1989**
This Japanese car can be driven on the road or over rough ground off the road. It has four-wheel drive, which means that the power of the engine is used to turn all four wheels.

**Holden 1958**
This Australian-built General Motors car was first introduced in 1948. It was cheap and tough and did not break down easily. Holdens are also sold in New Zealand, Africa, and Asia.

**Isotta Fraschini Type 8A 1925**

# Jaguar

### Jaguar E-Type 1963
This sports car, first sold in 1961 at less than half the price of similar models, was originally intended as a racing car. Its sleek shape was designed in a wind tunnel and it could go up to 150 mph (240 kph). More than half the E-types produced were sold in the United States.

Jaguar XK120 1950

## Kaiser Darrin 1954

Henry Kaiser was an American ship-builder who started making Kaiser-Fraser automobiles at the end of World War II. The company lasted only nine years, but it developed many new ideas. This roadster, for example, has doors that slide into the front fenders.

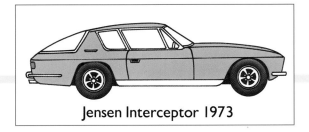

Jensen Interceptor 1973

# Lamborghini

## Lamborghini Countach 1985

People were thrilled by the Countach when it was first shown almost 20 years ago. It goes up to 180 mph (288 kph) and at the time was the world's fastest sports car. The spoiler on the back helps the car grip the road at very high speeds.

Lotus Esprit Turbo 1984

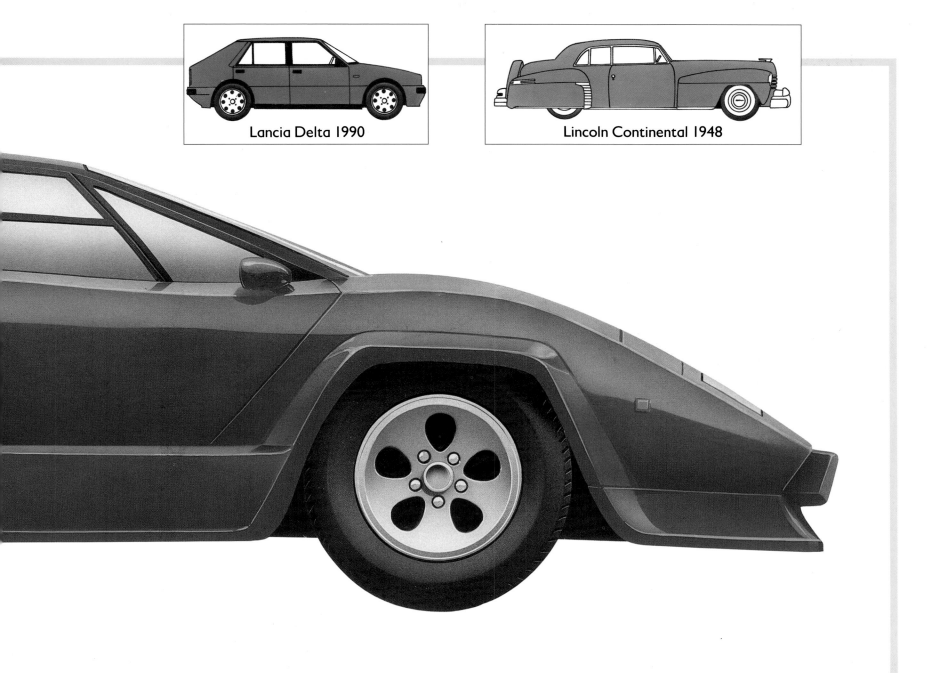

Lancia Delta 1990

Lincoln Continental 1948

# Mercedes-Benz

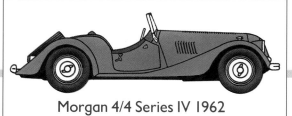

MG TC 1949

Morris Minor 1951

Morgan 4/4 Series IV 1962

**Mercedes-Benz 300SL Gullwing 1955**
Only 1,400 of these German sports cars were built 35 years ago. They were called Gullwing because the doors are hinged at the roof and open upwards.

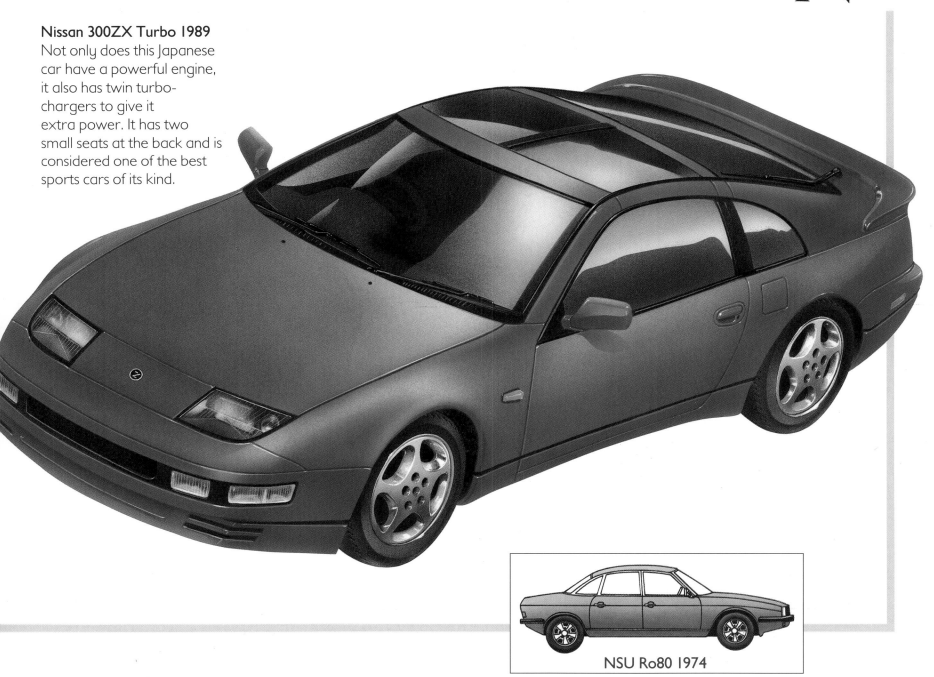

**Nissan 300ZX Turbo 1989**
Not only does this Japanese car have a powerful engine, it also has twin turbo-chargers to give it extra power. It has two small seats at the back and is considered one of the best sports cars of its kind.

NSU Ro80 1974

# Oldsmobile

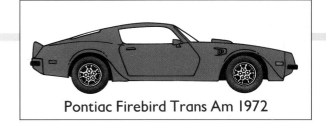

Pontiac Firebird Trans Am 1972

### Oldsmobile Cutlass Supreme 1967

Twenty years ago the Cutlass became one of America's favorite cars and the Supreme was the most popular Cutlass. At that time, the Supreme was a big heavy car. Smaller models were introduced at the end of the 1970s.

Opel Manta Berlinetta 1982

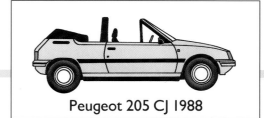

Peugeot 205 CJ 1988

## Quattro (Audi) 1980
Audi built their first Quattro in 1980. Its four-wheel drive helps it to corner at high speed without skidding. Its engine is turbocharged, giving it extra power and enough speed to reach 143 mph (229 kph).

## Porsche Carrera 1990
The Carrera was first built over 25 years ago as a racing sports car. The spoiler at the back was introduced in 1973 and helps the car grip the road at high speeds.

# Rolls-Royce

**Rolls-Royce Silver Spirit 1990**
The engine of this luxurious car is so smooth and quiet it seems to glide along. Rolls-Royce has been making such cars for nearly 90 years. A famous advertisement once claimed that when you rode in a Rolls-Royce, the only sound you could hear was the ticking of the clock.

Rover 820i Fastback 1989

Riley 1.5 1957

Reliant Scimitar 1970

Renault 5 TL Prima 1990

 Saab

### Saab 900 Turbo 1987

Saab was not the first company to use turbochargers, but it was the first to make them popular. The turbocharger uses the exhaust fumes to get extra power from the engine. Besides cars, Saab also makes airplanes.

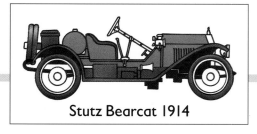

Stutz Bearcat 1914

Studebaker Avanti 1962

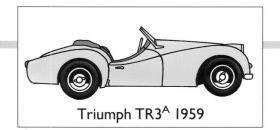

Triumph TR3$^A$ 1959

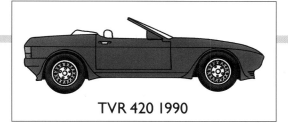

TVR 420 1990

## Toyota MR2 1990

This popular car comes from Japan. MR means the engine is placed in the middle to rear of the car. The 2 indicates that it seats only two people.

Sunbeam Alpine 1965

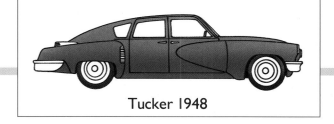

Tucker 1948

# Uno

**Uno (Fiat) 1990**

Fiat has been making cars for nearly
100 years. It is the biggest Italian
auto maker and the only one that
did not make its name with sports
cars. This small family car has a
hatchback or fifth door at the back.
This makes it easier to load
groceries and other things.

# Volkswagen

## Volkswagen "Beetle" 1968
The "Beetle" is the most popular car ever made. It was so cheap and reliable that 21 million were sold since it was first produced in Germany in 1938, over 50 years ago. "Beetles" are still being made today in Mexico.

**Volkswagen Golf GL 1990**

**Volvo 1800 ES 1972**

**Vauxhall Firenza 1974**

# Wolseley

**Wolseley Hornet MK1 1961**
This little car was first
produced in Britain about 30
years ago. It copied the Mini,
but was never as successful.
Although the Hornet went out
of production in 1970, the Mini
is still produced today.

Willys American 1941

**XJ-S (Jaguar) 1990**
Although the engine of this British
sports car is big and powerful, it is
also quiet and smooth. People like
the XJ-S for its fine control and
power. It seats four people and can
go up to 148 mph (233 kph).

# ale

## Yale 1905

This early American car, along with others of its period, was called a horseless carriage. The Yale's body, suspension, and even the shape of its seats, were like those of a horse-drawn vehicle. This car was thought to be so stylish it was called the Beau Brummel of the road, after the well-known British dandy.

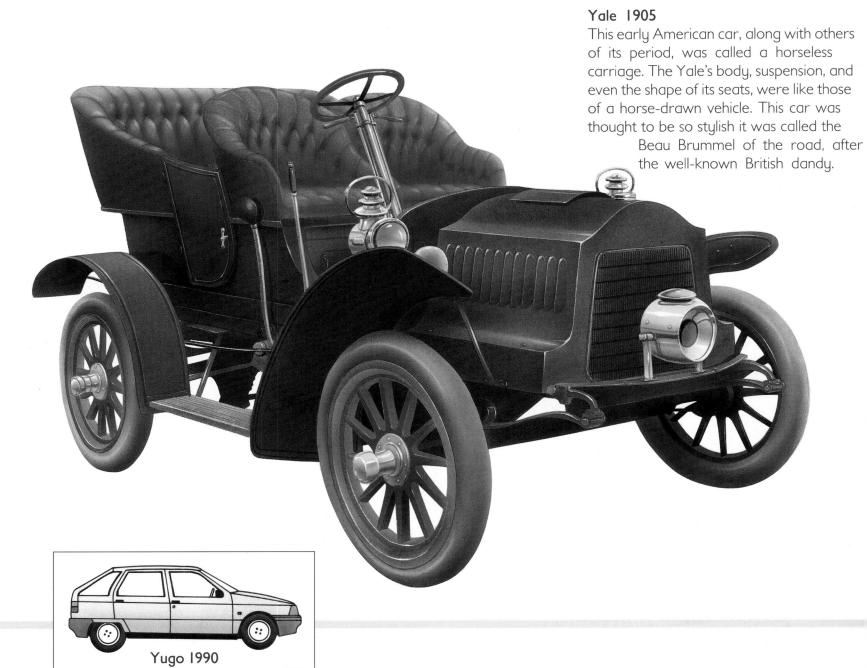

Yugo 1990

**Zephyr Zodiac (Ford) 1961**
The Zephyr Zodiac was made by Ford in Britain, both as the convertible shown here and as a four-door sedan. The design was influenced by the streamlined shape of the American Fords of the 1950s.

Zagato (Lancia) 1963

First edition for the United States, Canada, and the Philippines
published 1991 by Barron's Educational Series, Inc.

*The A-to-Z Book of Cars* was conceived, edited and designed by
Frances Lincoln Limited, Apollo Works, 5 Charlton Kings Road,
London, England.

*All inquiries should be addressed to:*
Barron's Educational Series, Inc.
250 Wireless Boulevard
Hauppauge, New York 11788
International Standard Book No. 0-8120-9267-8
International Standard Book No. 0-8120-6209-4
Library of Congress Catalog Card No. 90-19496

Library of Congress Cataloging-in-Publication Data

Royston, Angela
    The A-to-Z book of cars / Angela Royston, Terry Pastor. — 1st ed.
        p.      cm.
    Summary: Brief text and illustrations introduce twenty-six cars,
both classic and modern, from the Alfa Romeo Spider to the Zephyr
Zodiac.
    ISBN 0-8120-6209-4
    1. Automobiles – Juvenile literature.    [1. Automobiles.
2. Alphabet.]    I. Pastor, Terry.    II. Title.
TL147.R678    1991
629.222–dc20
[E]                                                              90-19496
                                                                    CIP
                                                                    AC

Printed and bound in Hong Kong
1234          987654321